# The

# Beginner's

# Guide

# to AI

David Rainey

Copyright © 2021 by David Rainey
All rights reserved.

Simultaneously published in United States of America, the UK, India, Germany, France, Italy, Canada, Japan, Spain, and Brazil.

No part of this book may be reproduced in any form or by any other electronic or mechanical means – except in the case of brief quotations embodied in articles or reviews – without written permission from its author.

For all young adults, especially Gabriel and Alannah!

Also, to Ray Kurzweil and Peter Diamandis, who had the vision and will to create Singularity University, and who inspired me to dig deeper into AI.

Finally, this book is dedicated to Ben Levy at Bootstrap Labs for helping me stay on the cutting edge.

# Contents

*Preface* ............................................................................. 7
Introduction ..................................................................... 9
What Is AI? ..................................................................... 11
History of AI ................................................................... 17
AI and Gaming ............................................................... 22
AI and Virtual Assistants ................................................ 25
AI and Self-Driving ......................................................... 28
AI and Business ............................................................. 35
AI and Healthcare .......................................................... 42
AI and Robots ................................................................ 48
AI and Energy ................................................................ 53
AI and Agriculture .......................................................... 59
AI and Quantum Computing .......................................... 65
AI and 3D Printing .......................................................... 71
Conclusion ..................................................................... 78

# *Preface*

This book is written for the people who will soon run the world – the Millennials and Gen Z. It's also written for all of the people who were liberal arts majors or didn't even go to college. The Beginner's Guide to Ai is an introductory overview of AI.

In this book, we will talk about exponential technologies. AI is one of them, but so are a bunch of the others talked about in this book. What is an exponential technology? It is a technology that is improving at an exponential rate. What does that mean? Well, you've probably heard the Indian chess story about the king who challenged the traveling sage to a game of chess. When the sage was asked what he wanted if he won, he said a single grain of rice on the first square of the chessboard and doubling the amount on each subsequent square. After the sage won, the king brought in a bag of rice and quickly learned about exponential growth. By the 20th square, the king had to place 1,000,000 grains of rice. By the $40^{th}$ square, 1,000,000,000 grains of rice, and by the $64^{th}$ square enough rice to cover the country of India in 3 feet thick of rice. That's exponential growth!

So, what does it really mean, and why should 18–34-year old's care? According to virtually all the experts in the field of AI, massive unemployment is coming, up to 30-50% of working age adults. This vast unemployment will hit in the next 10-20 years, and young people need to be prepared for it. The first way to be prepared is to learn as much as possible about AI. Then you know what is coming. This book is intended to be that first step for our younger adults, and even mid-career folks who don't yet see the train in the tunnel.

Because this book is about exponential technologies, some of it will be out of date by the time it is completed and published.

# Introduction

I decided to write this book out of shock and dismay. In the Spring of 2018, I asked my son, who was going to be a junior in college the next year, if anyone at his fancy Ivy League school had talked to the students about AI. He was just finishing his sophomore year. The shock and dismay came when he said, "No". How could a university be so grossly negligent not to discuss with the student body the force that will dominate their adult lives? I found it simply incomprehensible. Believe it or not, he just finished all four years of liberal arts college without one word from the university about AI.

So, I decided to "take the bull by the horns" and write a short and simple introductory book to AI, specifically targeting high school, college students and young men and women in their twenties, but one that also would be accessible to the general public as well.

Why me? I have had a strong interest in science and space since I was a child, and in concert with that have extensively read current scientific literature, not only in space-related subjects like astrophysics, but also in computer science and medicine. In my work, I have been responsible for my companies' computer systems (among other things) for over 20 years and therefore read a lot to stay current and hopefully on the cutting edge. I had heard about AI for years in the literature that I read. Coincidentally, an old work acquaintance started up an AI venture fund and information clearing house focused on applied AI (Bootstrap Labs). I signed up to go to their 3$^{rd}$ conference in 2018 and was hooked. I continued to read a lot on the subject during the last two years and returned to their 4th conference in 2019, by which time I had already determined to write this book for the sake of the kids.

I do not intend this book to be exhaustive. In fact, I probably will leave a lot of things out that may not be necessary to a reader new to the topic. I hope that I'm able to explain a complex and demanding subject in a simple and straightforward way that sparks the interest of students and young men and women specifically, but also the general public.

Also, feel free to check out my YouTube Channel - "The AI Guide". I post Tuesdays and Saturdays on YouTube plus on breaking AI news on Facebook and Instagram. Additional free resources are available at www.davidtheaiguide.com also.

# What Is AI?

What is AI? AI is short for Artificial Intelligence. Artificial Intelligence basically means "the capability of a machine to imitate intelligent human behavior"[1]. The end game of AI work is called Artificial General Intelligence, or AGI, which means a machine that can artificially match full human intelligence. While this is the end game, AI is nowhere near this achievement yet.

AI was a term started in 1955 by John McCarthy[2], a research scientist at Dartmouth College. To say that this idea was ahead of its time would be a huge understatement. At the time that John coined the term, computers were relatively new. A typical computer would fill a huge room and only do routine calculations, like trying to solve standard mathematical problems. Back then, computers could not in any way even match human calculational capabilities. For reference, see the movie Hidden Figures. So, John was a visionary in the sense that he foresaw those computers would one day become highly sophisticated and might even eventually replicate the human mind. John McCarthy won numerous awards including the Turing Award[3] and the U.S. National Medal of Science[4]. He spent most of his teaching career at Stanford University.

In addition to John McCarthy, Marvin Minsky was also working on the very first versions of neural networks in the early 1950's but became disenchanted with them. Minsky

---

[1] Merriam-Webster Dictionary online
[2] www.computerhope.com/jargon/a/ai.htm
[3] https://www.britannica.com/topic/Turing-Award
[4] https://www.nsf.gov/od/nms/recipients.jsp

also won the Turing Award, even before McCarthy[5]. Alan Turing, the man who literally invented the modern computer during World War II and about whom the movie The Imitation Game was made, had written a paper previously in 1950 about Computing Machinery and Intelligence. Turing invented the Turing Test, where "a remote human interrogator, within a fixed time frame, must distinguish between a computer and a human subject based on their replies to various questions posed by the interrogator. By means of a series of such tests, a computer's success at "thinking" can be measured."[6] So, the idea of machines as potentially intelligent preceded John McCarthy, but he framed the idea in a way that captured the imagination of the public by calling it "artificial intelligence".

Over the last 70+ years, AI was mostly worked on at universities because of its difficult challenges. At times, professors and researchers working on AI were made fun of because no one believed that it was possible to succeed until relatively recently.[7] Many people working on AI did so in isolation or in small groups to little acclaim, trying to produce the breakthrough that would bring AI into the mainstream. As Dr. Robert H. Goddard of NASA famously said, "It is difficult to say what is impossible, for the dream of yesterday is the hope of today and the reality of tomorrow."

One of the biggest constraints to achieving AI of any kind has been computer processing power. AI takes a huge amount of processing power, and very few people had access to any large enough amount of it. The exceptions were the

---

[5] https://www.britannica.com/topic/Turing-Award
[6] https://www.britannica.com/technology/Turing-test
[7] Crevier, AI: The Tumultuous History of the Search for Artificial Intelligence, pg. 100-144

universities, the governments and the military and its associated industries, who had the money and resources to build the huge computers necessary to do these kinds of calculations. So, decades of work were done in academic and defense settings.

AI is programmed by what is called an algorithm.[8] An AI algorithm is a set of instructions that tells the computer what to do in a repetitive manner. AI algorithms are a specialized type of computer programming and are done by software engineers who have been trained in the special characteristics of AI algorithms. This type of programming was learned entirely in a research setting or on the job since there were no academic programs to teach doing AI algorithms until very, very recently. In fact, Carnegie Mellon launched the first degree in AI in May 2018.[9] So, knowledge in the field has been largely self-taught or passed by direct experience and teaching from generation to generation, either in academic, government or military environments.

The first type of AI invented is called Machine Learning. Machine learning very simply means to train an AI algorithm to do one task by repeating it many times until the task is learned by the machine. Machine learning algorithms build a mathematical model based on sample data, known as "training data", in order to make predictions or decisions.[10] Machine learning is also called "supervised learning" in that labeled data fed by a human is used to train the algorithm.

---

[8] Knuth, Donald (1968), "The Art of Computer Programming, Vol. 1"
[9] https://www.cmu.edu/news/stories/archives/2018/may/ai-undergraduate-degee.html
[10] Bishop, C.M. (2006), "Pattern Recognition and Machine Learning"

This type of AI can be used to perform a specific step in a manufacturing process, for example. A desired outcome can or cannot be programmed into the algorithm, providing directed or open results. Even though Machine Learning was a big breakthrough, its applications are somewhat limited to the accomplishment of one particular task. It is not able to "think" in the sense that people do. Machine Learning can "learn" from past experience (data sets) and use that knowledge to inform future decisions.[11] Machine Learning has now evolved to achieve significant results in various specialized settings.

A second type of AI is called a neural net, which is considered a subset of Machine Learning by some experts. It is essentially an artificial brain that is built up by layer upon layer of transistors, designed to mimic the function of the human brain. Neural nets had been tried previously as early as the 1950's, the first being the Perceptron by Frank Rosenblatt[12], but the needed computing power was simply not available at that time, so the early neural nets did not work. Researchers then went back to Machine Learning to try to improve it to be more generally applicable. However, success in extending the operation of Machine Learning to more general cases was limited.

The big breakthrough in AI recently was getting a neural net to really work properly. This achievement happened in 2012, although initial advances were made in 2009-10.[13] The

---

[11] Kaplan Andreas; Michael Haenlein (2018), "Siri, Siri in my Hand, who's the Fairest in the Land? On the Interpretations, Illustrations and Implications of Artificial Intelligence", Business Horizons, 62(1)
[12] https://the-learning-machine.com/article/ml/perceptron
[13] Clark, Jack, (8 December 2015), "Why 2015 was a Breakthrough Year in Artificial Intelligence", Bloomberg News

technologies needed to break through with neural nets were two: GPUs or cloud computing and big data. GPUs are very powerful processors originally used in gaming and later used for AI by the pioneer Geoff Hinton. Cloud computing is simply being able to rent a server, which is a large computer capable of processing and storing a big amount of data. Renting is much more affordable than buying one. Each server is very expensive and having to buy enough servers to drive a neural net is beyond the reach of most organizations. Cloud computing lets you expand your computer processing in an almost unlimited way for as short as a day. Having massive computing power become available in a flexible and cheap way was needed before neural nets would work, and cloud computing is now commonplace with huge companies like Amazon, Microsoft and Google all vying for market share.

The second big need was huge sets of data to train the neural nets to do what you wanted it to do. For example, AI is now used to read X-rays and can do it better than a human can. The training for the neural net to be able to perform this task was inputting millions and millions of x-rays with different conditions into the neural net. Computers can process a much bigger volume of data than a human can, so the more data you give it as examples, the more accurate the results of the algorithm. Based on a much larger data set, neural nets can then exceed human performance, which is based on more limited data absorption capability. Working neural nets are a huge breakthrough that greatly expands the potential applications of AI.

The world leaders in AI currently are the United States and China. Other significant players in AI are Canada and the United Kingdom. Many other countries or groups are currently greatly expanding the resources being put into AI. Examples are Google and Microsoft for companies, and the European Union, Russia and Israel. In very short order, much of the world will be working in this field given its ultimate potential and power. Of course, there are applications under development for both military and civilian use. A lot of debate is happening now about what the appropriate limits on using AI should be and emerging risks of not putting such limits in place now. AI could be used to create extremely dangerous weapons and computer systems. The EU just issued draft regulations to begin to put limits on the use of AI.

Potential applications of AI include factory automation, medical uses for diagnosis, treatment and surgery, autonomous vehicles, military uses, energy management and much more. Perhaps the most common AI currently in use is in cell phones (Siri, Google Assistant) or home AI like Alexa and Google Home. Voice activated calling, texting, e-mailing and others are current phone-based AI applications. Alexa can turn on lights, appliances and more in combination with interfacing devices at the electrical plug. Home AI can also answer questions like, "What are the nearest restaurants?", "How long will it take me to get to work?", and "Who is number 12 on the Chicago White Sox?". All these functions are very neat and user friendly but are still quite limited compared to what is possible. The fully responsive computer Jarvis in the Iron Man movie series is a great example of the direction that AI development efforts are moving towards. Future AI will basically run your entire home and work life for you. We shall talk shortly about specific areas where AI is being used or being developed for use, and the positives and negatives of using AI in each of these areas.

# History of AI

The history of AI is both long and short. Long because work has been done in this area since the 1950's. Short because everything changed between 2010 and 2015 with the first successful neural nets and the acceleration of machine learning techniques.

I have already mentioned John McCarthy of Dartmouth (later Stanford) and Marvin Minsky of MIT. The other "founders" of AI include Allen Newell and Herbert Simon of Carnegie Mellon and Arthur Samuel of IBM. They all got together at Dartmouth College in 1956 at a workshop to lay out the principles and programming for AI. This workshop marked the beginning of Machine Learning, and Arthur Samuel coined the term in 1959.[14] Machine Learning can be defined by its words, i.e., machines learning from data. Pretty quickly into the 1960's, Machine Learning moved in the direction of probabilities (math and statistics).[15] At the beginning, the goal was to pick the most likely outcome from a set of variables, i.e., prediction or deduction. During the acceleration of Machine Learning in this decade, the focus moved to include inference as well. This aspect of AI development mirrors human intelligence in that people use both deductive (predictive) and inductive (inferential) reasoning.

AI had a period of strong growth from the late 1950's to the early 1970's. During this period, the attempt to develop a neural net failed due to lack of adequate computing capacity, which was limited and very expensive during this time period.

---

[14] Samuel, Arthur (1959), "Some Studies in Machine Learning Using the Game of Checkers",
[15] Solomonoff, Ray J. (1964), "A Formal Theory of Inductive Inference, Part II", Information and Control, pages 224-254

With machine learning, work was done on gaming and probabilities, but a big thrust was the effort to create "general intelligence" (i.e., human) with it. These general intelligence efforts with machine learning were not successful again due to limited computing capacity, but more importantly the difficulty of creating an algorithm to mimic human mental abilities. Human thinking is quite complex, both deductive and inductive. Even today, AI experts believe that AGI (Artificial General Intelligence) is still years away. Because of these failures and too much hype, the first "AI Winter" set in from roughly the mid-1970's to 1980, a period where government and defense groups abandoned AI research. Results simply could not be delivered at the time that satisfied these funding groups. In addition, during the 1970's, there were serious economic problems in the U.S., with high inflation and unemployment as well as gas shortages caused by the Arab oil embargo, government funding for AI became limited.

There was another AI boom focused on Machine Learning through Expert Systems from 1980 into the late 1980's. Expert Systems again are what it sounds like, building a system to replicate a human expert in a specific subject. Because they originated in the mid-1960's and further developed during the 1970's, by the 1980's these Expert Systems were among the first successes with AI software. Expert Systems were databases with an inference engine to find relationships within the data. Some progress was made with Machine Learning during this period. Some Expert Systems became highly reliable in their narrow area. There was a computer called Lisp Machine that a lot of the effort during this period was tied to. Later, these systems migrated to the server-client architecture that replaced the single machines like the Lisp.

Many but not all Expert Systems were used in the medical field. Two examples of Expert Systems are Mycin and Dendral.[16] Mycin was in the medical field, and it was used to identify bacteria that can cause serious infections and recommend treatments. Dendral was in the chemistry field, and it was used to predict the chemical structure of a molecule based on its spectrograph (which light is reflected). While these systems worked well for their uses, they were very narrow in application. Funding groups wanted AI that was more generally applicable. Expert Systems proved to not really be capable of any generalized intelligence that would accomplish multiple tasks at once. Because of these shortcomings, the second AI Winter arrived and lasted from the late 1980's into the 1990's. So, there had been two boom and bust cycles by the time that the mid-1990's arrived.

What changed then was that Machine Learning researchers switched from trying to reproduce human intelligence to using AI to solve specific problems, and computational power started to increase dramatically into the 2000's, largely as a result of the advent of large data centers and later cloud computing but also GPUs, which are much more powerful processors. Machine Learning moved from being able to execute algorithms to do a narrow specific task to being given a large data set and asked to look for correlations. This was a fundamental change in approach. A big example of this type is loading a lot of data on symptoms of illness and asking the AI to predict which illness is occurring. Research into using AI for medical applications has existed since the beginning, but it did not mature until big data sets became available from greatly increased concentration of business in the medical

---

[16] https://www.geeksforgeeks.org/expert-systems/

field. With millions of patients for examples in each database, diagnosing illness became significantly easier. In addition, despite data protections for medical records like HIPAA, datasets are often made anonymous by removing names, dates of birth and social security numbers but maintaining the data file of symptoms and diagnosis. In this case, aggregation into truly huge datasets is available. Later, the advent of personal health trackers like Fitbit started producing an avalanche of data for AI's to explore.

Meanwhile, in 2015, the creation of the first powerful, working neural net really expanded AI back into its long-time second approach beyond the Machine Learning algorithms started as early as the 1960's. Neural nets require huge processing power (like the brain), and cloud computing provided that needed power on demand for the first time (no reliance anymore on your own limited data center). Neural nets still use algorithms, but they can be told up front what to look for out of a lot of data or be given a lot of data and asked for relationships within that data. Neural nets really focus more on inference within data, while traditional Machine Learning is more deductive (if these things exist then this happens). Attempts at inference had been around for many years going back to the Bayesian networks, which was coined in 1985 by Judea Pearl but bounded in 1997 by Luby and Dagum to a degree that allowed practical implementation for use with AI. Like so much else in the field of AI, discovery and implementation of inference really took off in the late 1990's. The twenty years from 1995 to 2015 was a watershed era for making AI a more practical reality. It was Geoff Hinton and the PHD's that he trained that made the breakthrough in 2012 at the ImageNet

computer vision conference where a neural net for the first time beat the existing machine learning based systems.[17]
AI development since 2015 has entered the exponential phase. There are now near daily breakthroughs or stories about new applications of AI that are changing life for the betterment of humanity. A current example of the use of AI by NASA to analyze the flood of data coming from satellites today. With the advent of commercial launch companies like SpaceX and Rocket Lab, new satellites are being put up monthly, and the volume of data coming back is enormous. No human or group of humans could hope to make practical use of all of it, so NASA is programming AI's to analyze the data to find key factors driving certain events, like hurricanes. NASA just released a story about using AI to better identify the hurricanes that rapidly increase in strength before landfall, making this type of hurricane particularly dangerous. AI recently identified three key factors that cause a hurricane to rapidly intensify, and now the algorithms are 60%+ more accurate in forecasting these hurricanes, leading directly to lives that will be saved from these storms.[18] Use of AI is now becoming routine in scientific research, dramatically improving and accelerating the benefits of that research.

So, this is why I stated at the opening of the chapter that the history of AI is both long and short. AI research has been going on since the 1960's, followed by two periods of disillusionment, and ultimate development and implementation in the late 1990's and 2000's.

---

[17]https://www.pcmag.com/news/the-ai-breakthrough-will-require-researchers-burying-their-hatchets
[18] https://www.nasa.gov/feature/jpl/a-machine-learning-assist-to-predicting-hurricane-intensity

# AI and Gaming

One of the original applications of AI from the 1950's was in Gaming. Gaming was a natural first avenue for the development of AI. Teach an AI to play a simple game like checkers as a player, for example. Games with set rules allowed an AI programmer to develop the initial logic that has become the hallmark of AI. Because of rules, many steps of "if-then" could be programmed. Over time, AI's became better players at simple games that did not have a lot of rules and variability. Checkers was a natural in this regard, and initial success in checkers occurred early in the 1960's.

The next game that AI researchers attempted to program was chess. Chess has much more complexity than checkers, so it was much more difficult to program an AI to master. Initial attempts in the 1960's and 1970's failed, probably due to lack of adequate processing power. Then came the first AI winter. In the 1980's, IBM began developing an AI to play chess at the Watson Research Center. Also, in the 1980's, world champion Garry Kasparov was at the height of his career. IBM decided to develop an AI capable of defeating Kasparov. Such a victory would signal AI's maturity into a viable tool.

IBM first developed Deep Thought, which played Kasparov in 1989 for the first time. Kasparov won both games against Deep Thought. IBM did not give up though. In 1996, IBM completed Deep Blue, which played Kasparov in a six-set match. Kasparov won four games to two. This match marked the first game ever lost by a world champion to a computer program. This result showed that significant progress had been made in the development of a sophisticated AI. In 1997, just one year later, Deep Blue beat Kasparov in a rematch 3.5

games to 2.5 games (the half games were ties). Following this watershed event, AI research really took off. Today, the world chess champion cannot win a match against an AI.[19]

Following Deep Blue's victory, AI's were developed to play many other games including Scrabble. However, the next major level of AI gaming development regarded the game Go. Go is considered a much more difficult game than chess even though on the surface it is simpler. From 1997, researchers gradually worked on an AI to play go, but it was very difficult. A company called Deep Mind was founded in 2010 to work toward Artificial General Intelligence (AGI), which is human cognitive capability. As you recall, the first viable neural nets were developed between 2010 and 2015, and Deep Mind was a player in this sector. Deep Mind's progress was significant enough that Google bought them in 2014. Deep Mind was developing an AI during this period called Alpha Go. In October 2016, Deep Mind arranged for Alpha Go to play Fan Hui, the European Go champion. Alpha Go defeated Hui 5-0, a shocking development that many thought would not happen for years.[20] This event demonstrated the rapid progression of AI from 2010 to 2016.

Even though using AI to play games is quite old, going back to the 1960's, using AI to facilitate a person playing a game is very new. Surprisingly, the first game to incorporate AI into the game itself is *very* recent. Nvidia announced it in December 2018 as a game demonstration using AI for

---

[19] https://becominghuman.ai/the-history-of-chess-ai-f8b0dcb4d6d4
[20] https://www.wired.com/2016/01/in-a-huge-breakthrough-googles-ai-beats-a-top-player-at-the-game-of-go/

graphics in a driving scene. The AI was used to render the video images to make them look more realistic.[21]

Simple AI is used in many games to control non-player things like animals, etc., but it is quite simple and not like the AI discussed in the other chapters of this book. Much of what has been used in games until very recently is basically decision trees that get more and more sophisticated. One of the reasons for limited use of AI like a neural net in games is because it would slow the game down.[22] Remember that neural nets typically take a lot of computing power. So, these earlier decision tree based simple AI's were the state of the art until 2020.

In 2020, OpenAI introduced the Gym in Super Mario Brothers. The Gym is a true neural net with options scaled down so as not to slow down the gaming experience. The Gym provides dynamic challenges to the player without overwhelming them.[23] Besides the challenge of limiting the AI's options to reduce computation, using an AI in games is also constrained by not introducing an unbeatable opponent or environment. Gamers would quickly lose interest in any game where they simply couldn't win.

---

[21] https://www.theverge.com/2018/12/3/18121198/ai-generated-video-game-graphics-nvidia-driving-demo-neurips
[22] https://towardsdatascience.com/artificial-intelligence-in-video-games-3e2566d59c22
[23] https://pypi.org/project/gym-super-mario-bros/

# AI and Virtual Assistants

An area of serious focus using AI has been personal or virtual assistant software. Siri was the first and was introduced by Apple in October 2011. Now there are many of these tools. Other popular ones today are Amazon's Alexa and Google Assistant. Microsoft has Cortana, but Amazon and Google dominate the market. Siri has fallen behind others as Apple has focused more on its hardware than its software.

Virtual/personal assistants can handle a wide variety of tasks now just nine years after its introduction. Many of these assistants are now found in people's homes. The home hardware includes Google Home and Amazon Echo as well as many others. The hardware provides the internet gateway to the AI assistant, and the assistant is housed on Google's or Amazon's servers in a remote location like a lot of software today.

Some of the tasks that virtual assistants are used for include managing your calendar, maintaining your shopping list, checking the movies in your area, weather forecasts, traffic on your commute, answering questions that you used to have to look up the answers for online or in a book, as an alarm clock, and a lot more. The capabilities of these assistants were limited initially but are very rapidly becoming more and more useful. For example, I use my Echo at home to ask what the names of people on sports teams are by their uniform number, for adding things to my shopping list, for weather, for my commute and of course for playing music. You can also use Alexa with smart plugs to turn or turn off lights, adjust your thermostat for heating or air conditioning, or keeping track of what's in your refrigerator in the most modern ones. Much of these activities were the stuff of science fiction not long ago.

The sophistication of virtual assistants is in its infancy still. If you want to know where things are heading, think "Jarvis" in the Iron Man movies. Jarvis can independently analyze a problem and develop a solution to it. The future AI virtual assistant will track your family members and let you know where they are and when they will be home based on their calendar and traffic. It will know your favorite foods and always keep them in stock through your shopping list. Eventually, the AI will, with the help of robotics, be able to cook your dinner and clean up afterward. The largest single future impact of these sophisticated AI will be to free up your time. What will you do with the time that you now must use to cook, clean, do laundry, shop and all the other mundane chores of life that will go away in 5-10 years? Will you use it productively, or will you just let it go by? This question will become a principal challenge to humanity in the future.

Virtual assistants will also plan all your vacations based on your interests. They will offer you courses to take so that you can learn new knowledge or skills. They will remind you to pick up your dry cleaning, schedule and book your hair appointment (which it can already do), tell you what is going on in your town that day and plan your night out with your friends, including tickets and reservations. And don't forget the kids – lessons, games, friends – their whole schedule. All of it will appear on your phone without any effort by you. Need a new car? Your assistant will show you a wide variety of options and find the one with the best price within a reasonable drive. It will also contact the dealer and set an appointment to test drive the car and one day arrange the financing for you based on your bank balances and credit score, sending the down payment and an electronic signature so that you arrive at the dealership and are handed the keys.

Does it all sound farfetched? Not at all, Toyota Research is working right now to perfect a robot that can do all household chores. It will be fully functional within a few years, but it can already unload the dishwasher and put the dishes in the cabinet. The robot is taught using Virtual Reality to do these tasks by a human instructor. AI is what drives the robot's learning ability. Machine Learning lets the robot learn in only one try. Once one robot learns a task, it is shared with all the other robots in Toyota's robot fleet.[24] Why would Toyota work on something like this outside of their car business? So older people can stay in their homes as they age and still drive and buy cars I suppose! "Robot, don't forget to let the dog in!" How's that for a personal assistant?

One of the coolest future uses of AI-driven assistants, at least to me, is to make the computer keyboard fully obsolete. As voice recognition continues to improve, the day will come when you no longer need type anything. You can already use Siri or Google Assistant to type your text messages and e-mails on your phone. However, voice recognition still makes quite a few errors. And what about laptops and desktops? The goal would be able to just speak to your computer and never type, which the AI would do with near 100% accuracy. That would be fantastic! Microsoft Office has Dictate, but what I am describing is more sophisticated, much like Jarvis in Iron Man. AI will do it soon, and it will be error free. That voice recognition works at all with everyone's different accent, speaking tempo and varying use of language is already amazing!

---

[24] https://www.engadget.com/2019/10/04/toyota-research-institute-robots-vr-training/?guccounter=1

# AI and Self-Driving

The AI-driven revolution (pun intended) in transportation is already well underway. AI works today in many cars with both Lane Assist to keep your car in your lane and also Adaptive Cruise Control that speeds up and slows down based on traffic. Of course, these technologies work because of AI but also due to other emergent technologies like Lidar, which is laser-based radar (rather than sound-based radar as traditionally used). In this sense, AI is converging with other technologies to make modern wonders happen. Convergence of different technologies is a very powerful force today. I first heard about technology convergence from Peter Diamandis, the founder of the XPrize and the co-founder of Singularity University. Peter is one of the most plugged in, knowledgeable people today about emerging technologies.

<u>Trucks</u>

However, in the transportation area, AI use is just beginning compared to what the future will bring. Let's start with trucking. Did you know that there is a shortage of about 30,000 long haul truck drivers in the U.S. in 2019? This is because long haul trucking is hard. Long hours, long trips and often being away from home are the drawbacks, despite pay today of around $80,000 a year gross. Since the economy was good for many years now up until Covid, and the trucker shortage has also existed for many years, what is the AI solution to that? Autonomous trucks. Semi-autonomous trucks with safety drivers intervening and correcting have been on the road since as far back as 2014 (Mercedes). In fact, Otto (part of Uber that was closed in July 2018) did the first driver-assisted run on public roads in October 2016 for

Budweiser from Denver to Colorado Springs.[25] The first fully autonomous run not on public roads was done by Volvo in November 2018. Then, in May 2019, Einride out of Sweden did the first fully autonomous (no driver) run in the world on public roads.[26] Then, just one month later in June 2019, Starsky Robotics did the first run of a fully autonomous truck in the U.S.[27] All autonomous truck runs to date have been in rural areas, mostly on freeways going from an entry exit to a departing exit. At the same time, Boxbot is working on fully autonomous delivery of local freight.[28] Local freight is handled door-to-door by much smaller trucks. Finally, on September 9, 2019, Freightliner (owned by Daimler/Mercedes) began the first Level 4 autonomous truck shipments in rural southwest Virginia in partnership with Torc Robotics, Daimler's autonomy partner.[29] Level 4 autonomy means that the truck drives by itself but has a human safety driver. Torc has successfully tested the system under a variety of adverse conditions including snow, rain and fog. As an alternative to Level 4 autonomy, a company called Peloton from the Bay Area is testing platooning trucks using automation.[30] Platoons of trucks follow very closely behind each other thereby saving fuel. Peloton believes that its platooning technology will be commercially viable sooner than Level 4 or 5 autonomy. Other truck companies working

---

[25] https://www.computerworld.com/article/3134879/self-driving-18-wheeler-delivers-the-first-shipment-beer.html
[26] https://www.gearbrain.com/autonomous-truck-startup-companies-2587305809.html
[27] https://www.trucks.com/category/news/tech/autonomous-vehicles/
[28] https://www.trucks.com/2019/06/06/boxbot-rautonomous-delivery-system/
[29] https://www.trucks.com/2019/09/09/daimler-starts-highway-test-autonomous-freightliner-truck/
[30] https://www.trucks.com/2019/07/17/peloton-robot-platooning-trucks/

on autonomy include Embark, TuSimple (recently purchased by UPS), Waymo and Tesla.[31] Most recently, Einride started providing Coca-Cola European Partners in Sweden with a fully autonomous truck to ferry goods from CCEP's warehouse to a large customer's warehouse, partly over public roads.[32]

So, autonomous trucking has made significant progress in only five years but still faces significant challenges. Remaining challenges include autonomy on congested freeways, off of freeways on local streets and delivery or pickup at loading docks. Full Level 5 autonomy, with no human in the cab, is still a number of years off for these more difficult challenges.[33] However, it's not hard to imagine that terminal to terminal runs along long stretches of freeway may happen within the next few years. Given that people in regular cars can't see that well into a truck cab because of its height, most initial autonomy will not be noticeable to other drivers going in the same direction. Once autonomous truck companies solve the problem of operating on local streets, autonomous trucks will be much more noticeable to oncoming traffic and pedestrians.

Cars and SUV's

How about passenger cars and SUV's? Think that autonomous cars are a new idea? Well, no. Inventor Francis Houdina drove a remote-controlled car through the streets of

---

[31] https://www.gearbrain.com/autonomous-truck-startup-companies-2587305809.html
[32] https://www.freightwaves.com/news/coca-cola-to-deploy-av-electric-transport-vehicle-in-sweden
[33] https://emerj.com/ai-adoption-timelines/self-driving-trucks-timelines/

Manhattan all the way back in 1925. Fast forward to 1969, when John McCarthy, one of the founding fathers of AI mentioned in Chapter 2, wrote an essay on a computer-controlled car using a TV camera to "see". In the early 1990's, Carnegie-Mellon researcher Dean Pomerleau wrote a PhD about using a neural net to provide self-driving for a car, and then took his net on the road for a hands-free drive from Pittsburgh to San Diego (the gas and brakes were human operated).[34] In 2002, DARPA (the Defense Advanced Research Projects Agency) offered a $1 million prize to the company that could autonomously drive a 142-mile course. The Grand Challenge was held in 2004, and all participants failed the challenge. The next day, DARPA announced a second Grand Challenge a year and a half after the first one. This time, five teams completed the course, with Stanford University winning it.[35]

During the 2000's, car features such as parking and lane assist and backup cameras were invented, which were partial, early steps toward autonomous cars. Such features are called Level 1 automation and helped develop camera systems needed for autonomy. In 2009, Google started its self-driving car project that eventually became Waymo. By 2013, the major car manufacturers had all jumped in and started their own autonomous vehicle projects. Millions of miles have now been driven autonomously with a human safety driver present. One interesting question is how many miles are needed for the machine learning algorithms to exceed human driver safety standards. In January 2018, Nvidia unveiled an AI chip for cars called Xavier and is partnering with VW.

---

[34] https://www.digitaltrends.com/cars/history-of-self-driving-cars-milestones/
[35] https://www.darpa.mil/news-events/2014-03-13

Other efforts to implement AI into vehicles are underway by the other major car companies.[36]

The goal is to get autonomous cars to become safer than human drivers. Because driving is such a complex task, it is taking longer than expected. There have been fatalities caused by vehicles in autonomous mode. Five of them have been Tesla drivers not paying attention as required in Level 2 mode (driver assisted), and one was a pedestrian fatality with an Uber Volvo in Level 3 mode (conditional automation).[37] There have been no fatalities yet with Level 4 or Level 5 automation. Any fatalities are bad, but we should consider that over 40,000 fatalities a year occur caused by human drivers, which is a very high number by comparison.

<u>Other transportation projects</u>

A major effort underway for autonomous transport (driven by AI) is what they call "last mile" delivery. This is basically delivery of packages in a small town or city, or a part of a larger city. The goal is to supplement the human element in delivering the millions of packages arriving on doorsteps daily. To put the size of the package delivery business into perspective, UPS alone has more than 399,000 employees in the US delivering documents and packages.[38] What if even a fraction of those folks could be replaced by automation?

One example is Starship Technologies, founded by the co-founders of Skype. In January 2019, 25 robotic couriers

---

[36] https://www.digitaltrends.com/cars/history-of-self-driving-cars-milestones/
[37] https://en.wikipedia.org/wiki/List_of_self-driving_car_fatalities
[38] https://pressroom.ups.com/pressroom/ContentDetailsViewer.page?ConceptType=FactSheets&id=1426321563187-193

started delivering food to students at George Mason University through Starship's partnership with Sodexho for only $1.99.[39] The robots can recharge, cross streets, climb curbs, deliver at night and work in bad weather. Starship had already started a similar service on the Intuit campus a year before. They also started a $10 per month package delivery service for small business and consumers. During the coronavirus pandemic, they have started selling their robots to restaurants to deliver food.

Starship has a lot of competition, with the biggest challenge directly from UPS and FedEx, but also from Postmates, Marble, Dispatch and Robby. FedEx debuted their robot in February 2019[40], and UPS is working with partners on drone delivery and robotics. Postmates launched their delivery robot in 2018 in L.A. and continue to roll it out in test environments.[41] Marble has been delivering food in San Francisco since 2017.[42] Amazon acquired Dispatch in 2017 to bring talent in house for development of its Scout delivery robot.[43] Dispatch had previously tested its Carry robot on two California college campuses, including Menlo College. Robby is building snack delivery bots for Pepsico.[44] Other robotic delivery companies include Segway, Nuro and Kiwi. This segment for robots will grow very, very quickly during the next 10 years.

---

[39] https://venturebeat.com/2019/01/22/starship-technologies-robots-begin-delivering-food-to-college-kids/
[40] https://about.van.fedex.com/newsroom/thefuturefedex/
[41] https://serve.postmates.com/
[42] https://www.marble.io/
[43] https://techcrunch.com/2019/02/07/meet-the-tiny-startup-that-helped-build-amazons-scout-robot/
[44] https://robby.io/

Like all other AI-driven technology, delivery robots are relatively new, and all sprang up since 2015, with most setting up shop in 2016 after Starship unveiled it prototype back in 2015. So, there is already a lot of competition in the last-mile delivery space that will drive innovation and lead to rapid improvement and deployment of these technologies. Most of these companies have top AI, robotics and computer vision people who jumped from larger companies in related sectors like Google, Microsoft, Boston Dynamics and others. As with all new business models, some will survive and some will fail, but it difficult to tell who will come out on top in the early stages of development of this business.

# AI and Business

AI will change work greatly in the future. For large companies, AI is already playing a big role. For smaller companies, not so much yet. However, as AI continues to mature and simplify, even smaller companies will eventually start to use it as AI becomes easier to use and cheaper.

Robotics

Robotics in manufacturing have been around for a long time now. The first industrial robot was created by George Devol (who also invented the barcode) back in 1954, and a patent was issued in 1961. George partnered with Joseph Engelberger to develop and market his invention. Joseph was eventually so successful that he became known as the "Father of Robotics". Their first robot was installed in a GM die casting plant in New Jersey in 1961.[45] George and Joe's Unimate robot soon took over the die casting industry.

In 1969, Joe got his shot on the automotive assembly line. GM was automating the plant at Lordstown, Ohio. The Unimate was put right on the main assembly line spot welding major pieces of the cars to form the body after the parts were placed by employees.[46] At the time, GM almost doubled the previous rate of production to 110 cars per hour, far and away the fastest at the time. Now, most automobile assembly plants are highly automated, with very few humans on the main assembly line as robots can pick up major parts

---

[45] https://www.roboticsbusinessreview.com/manufacturing/the_first_industrial_robot_why_it_failed/
[46] https://www.robotics.org/joseph-engelberger/unimate.cfm

of the car, put them in place and then weld them to secure them.

Use of robots also quickly spread globally at the end of the 1960's and into the 70's. For example, in 1967 a European company developed a specialized robot to do spray painting. This company later became ABB, which is one of the largest companies in the world and continues to have a robotics business.[47] In the 1970's and 80's, use of robots expanded into other industries and completely different fields of endeavor, such as assisting handicapped persons. A huge surge in investment in robotics happened in the 1980's in the US, but capabilities did not match expectations, and a prolonged contraction in robotics revenue lasted from the late 1980's all the way to the 2010's.[48] During the downturn, robotics companies disappeared from the US and were exclusively overseas companies until 2010. These periods of growth and retraction mirror the early days of AI as discussed in Chapter 2.

Robotics has moved far beyond the factory floor. Very far. For example, robotic spacecraft have explored the Moon, Mars and asteroids at ground level, and have explored the whole solar system from space. Space has become a big venue for robotics, including recently on the International Space Station to help the astronauts run the station in the form of two free-flying robots from Astrobee.[49] Also, the space station has long had the Dextre robot arm to help with maintenance tasks on the outside of the station. The

---

[47] https://new.abb.com/news/detail/19429/abb-names-peter-voser-as-interim-ceo
[48] https://www.robots.com/articles/industrial-robot-history
[49] https://techcrunch.com/2019/11/26/nasas-second-free-flying-assistant-robot-gets-to-work/

Canadarm is the premier robot arm that helps astronauts when working outside the space station and also helps dock supply ships to the station.[50]

Lately, the cost of robots is plummeting. I an executive in the aerospace industry, and we have been actively evaluating robots for our manufacturing operations. We use specialized machines to cut and shape components for sale to our customers. We looked at a robot to help load and unload our machines with parts to be processed. A robot that we looked at in the fall of 2017 that cost $80,000 at that time had dropped in cost to $50,000 only 18 months later, so robots are not only getting more sophisticated, but they are also getting much cheaper and easier to deploy.

Where does AI fit into robotics? I am glad that you asked. Without AI, robots can only follow a limited set of instructions defined by a human. The human can send new instructions to the robot through a computer interface, but in all circumstances without AI the human must continually direct the robot. AI, specifically machine learning or a neural net, allows a robot to "learn" and ultimately determine for itself what the best way is to complete a particular task. As mentioned earlier, the robot is given an objective and then allowed to figure out the best way to reach the objective using AI. I will talk more about robotics in Chapter 8.

AI at Work Today

AI is already in the workplace today. Most companies use Microsoft products like Office to write e-mails, letters, product information and much more, or to do spreadsheets

---

[50] https://asc-csa.gc.ca/eng/canadarm/default.asp

or presentations. Microsoft's e-mail application, Outlook, now has Insights, which is an AI-driven application to help manage most people's high volume of work e-mail by flagging what or who is most important and helping you to have focus time without e-mail or alerts interrupting.[51] Even better, it automatically sorts e-mail between important and time-wasting. Also, Microsoft's MyAnalytics tells you how you actually work in terms of how much time you spend in each application, how focused that time is and how you can improve your time management. So, this is an early and limited AI to act as your assistant.

Similarly, Word has Dictate, which is a speech recognition AI to allow you to speak your writing rather than typing out everything.[52] Eventually, this type of speech recognition ability will be integrated into many things, allowing you to do virtually any work by speaking rather than typing, except perhaps for design work. Imagine how much faster you can get your work done each day by dictating it all rather than typing. This capability is a real efficiency improvement, and I have already discussed how Siri, Google Assistant, Alexa and other applications do this outside of work, or as an enhancement to work for search functions.

AI is already being heavily used in Human Resources at larger companies. Most large companies now use AI to screen resumes since they get thousands of resumes every day. However, using AI to screen resumes has been controversial. Applicants hate feeling like a machine is deciding their job fate. Companies like Amazon are scrapping it due to biases

---

[51] https://docs.microsoft.com/en-us/workplace-analytics/insights-in-outlook
[52] https://www.microsoft.com/en-us/garage/profiles/dictate/

occurring in the machine learning process.[53] However, Amazon is the exception rather than the rule, and applicants can expect to be exposed to AI screening at more and more companies going forward.

AI is being used in other HR related functions in companies at this time. One of the most prominent new uses is Chatbots, which are AI to carry on conversations with applicants, employees and customers. Chatbots are an extension of Natural Language Processing (NLP – think Siri).[54] Chatbots are being used to report harassment, enhancing the new employee experience and even recommending career paths to employees.[55]

AI in manufacturing is changing logistics through warehouse automation, improving quality through better sensors and streamlining supply chains (all the things needed to make other things) through prediction and automation. Better sensors in warehouse robots make them safer while making them more autonomous (just like cars and trucks). Better sensors in manufacturing is best expressed by the term IoT, or Internet of Things. IoT is basically connecting any device to the internet and through that to networks of other devices and software.[56] These manufacturing IoT sensors can be used to improve quality through scanning at very small scales. Using AI in purchasing software allows it to predict upcoming needs based on market conditions, supplier

---

[53] https://www.reuters.com/article/us-amazon-com-jobs-automation-insight-idUSKCN1MK08G
[54] https://expertsystem.com/chatbot/
[55] https://www.forbes.com/sites/emilyhe/2019/06/20/ai-at-work-where-are-we-now-and-where-are-we-going/#584e7de9432e
[56] https://www.ibm.com/blogs/internet-of-things/what-is-the-iot/

conditions, and even weather and political events.[57] Finally, AI is being used to predict when machinery will need maintenance and what type it will need.

Use of AI in manufacturing is still in its infancy, with many large and especially mid-size and smaller companies not even using it yet due to cost and programming requirements. Currently, a large and expensive IT staff is needed to effectively use AI. As the cost drops and programming is improved through better language processing capability, AI will get much easier and more affordable to use. Once it is easier and cheaper, adoption will accelerate dramatically. Some believe that it will allow highly customized production in quantities as small as an individual consumer in the future. Chapter 12 talks about this kind of manufacturing. Only time will tell what happens.

## HCI – Human-Computer Interface

Perhaps the biggest eventual impact on the nature of work will be driven by the development and perfection of a human (brain) – computer interface, or BCI. What does this mean? Instead of speaking to put something on your shopping list, you just think it. What would life be like with this amazing technology in place? How much time would this functionality save you each day?

For work, this technology would eliminate the need for keyboards and typing as we know it today. A person's thoughts would be transcribed directly to a word processor to create documents. Also, presentations could be imagined and produced in real time. No more translation through a clunky

---

[57] https://www.autodesk.com/redshift/future-of-artificial-intelligence/

physical interface whether keyboard or mouse or pen. It would be Jarvis from Iron Man but without even speaking.

Interestingly, this AI technology is for human enhancement rather than human replacement. This is the positive side of AI to increase human abilities. What if you could have the sum total of human knowledge instantly accessible to you? What innovations would happen because of this technology? Eventually, the technology could be very democratizing if it's available to anyone in the world, and BCI may reward people for their creativity directly through the power of invention. One thing is for sure, and that is that if things in life seem fast now, it would be blindingly fast in this environment. We'll talk more about BCI in the next chapter.

# AI and Healthcare

AI is already being used in healthcare, and in the next ten years AI-driven research will make a huge impact on current challenges in the medical field. Use of AI in healthcare is being driven by two converging forces: a) an explosion in healthcare data from digitizing health records and the huge adoption of trackers that many people are wearing now; and b) rapid improvements in AI algorithms used to analyze this new flood of data.

Electronic healthcare records (EHR) and electronic medical records (EMR) go back to at least the early 1960's, when the Mayo Clinic in Cleveland and others launched early projects to digitize healthcare records. These first efforts were very expensive, so adoption was super slow. As late as 2001, only 18% of doctors were using EHR's. [58] While most doctors now use electronic records, there are many different systems on the market, and most of them do not talk with each other. That creates a problem when people want to move from one doctor to another, so usually paper records are still sent to the new doctor.

EHR and EMR are natural candidates for the use of AI, but it is very recent. At the big healthcare IT conference in March 2018, major vendors were just starting to implement AI into their EHR platforms.[59] One of the main uses of AI will be to standardize data so that it can be shared across platforms. Also, AI is starting to make clinical recommendations to some doctors based on test results, but this capability is still

---

[58] https://www.beckershospitalreview.com/healthcare-information-technology/a-history-of-ehrs-10-things-to-know.html
[59] https://www.healthcareitnews.com/news/next-ehrs-vendors-adding-artificial-intelligence-workflow

in its early stages. As algorithms improve and data available continues to increase, AI-driven doctor guidance should start to increase rapidly over the next ten years.

Perhaps the leading area where AI is in widespread use now is in radiology to read x-rays, MRI's and other images like CT and PET. Images are what is called structured data because they are always in the same format, so you can feed the Deep Learning models very large datasets so that they can learn what to look for.[60] The reliability of AI image analysis now has surpassed that of human radiologists for some tests. As the datasets grow, the rate of further improvement will increase significantly. As John Maeda points out in his book, "How to Speak Machine", computers can learn exponentially, where humans cannot. Historically, medical specialists read and interpreted patient images. Specialists built skill through repetitive experience. Deep Learning, an advancement in neural nets and how the layers interact, works the same way. Thousands to millions of images are fed to the Deep Learning algorithm, and the AI learns to read the images with great accuracy. The primary focus of AI in radiology has been with cancer but is starting to expand to neurological and digestive tract images more recently.[61] As you can see, the ability to reference millions of images easily surpasses human ability.

In addition to radiology, medical diagnosis has become a major application area for AI. Diagnosis is a good area because the symptoms can be categorized and then become analyzed by Deep Learning algorithms. For a given disease, the programmers can give the AI thousands of patient visits for that disease, and over time the AI begins to recognize the

---

[60] https://svn.bmj.com/content/2/4/230
[61] https://www.ncbi.nlm.nih.gov/pmc/articles/PMC6268174/

symptoms, sometimes better than human doctors. Recent Danish and Chinese testing of Deep Learning algorithms showed results better than humans in correctly identifying heart attacks in progress during 911 calls and in predicting the spread of breast cancer.[62] Since AI is really just being integrated into health record systems (EHR/EMR), its skill at diagnosis should increase sharply over the next decade based on the trend of results to date. Again, AI can exponentially improve results over time, gradually matching human diagnostic skill and eventually surpassing it. A current example of this technology is Buoy Health, which is now in use at Harvard Health and others to intake patients and diagnose them.[63] Technology like this will become commonplace at most healthcare offices and centers in the next five years.

One of the most fascinating possibilities for medical diagnosis and treatment is the prospect of nanobots flowing through your bloodstream, looking for problems and eventually repairing them. How cool is that? For example, DNA robots are in testing that will find pre-cancer or cancer cells and destroy them on the spot.[64] Another possibility of nanobots is drug delivery right at the site needed, which virtually eliminates side effects. Ultimately, the nanobots may help you live a very, very long time. Would you want to live to 150? These steps with nanobots may be considered the first toward becoming a hybrid being between human and machine. Would you want that? Finally, Ray Kurzweil, the

---

[62] https://www.forbes.com/sites/bernardmarr/2018/07/27/how-is-ai-used-in-healthcare-5-powerful-real-world-examples-that-show-the-latest-advances/#e2c01535dfbe
[63] https://www.buoyhealth.com/#solutions
[64] https://interestingengineering.com/nanobots-will-flowing-body-2030

eminent futurologist and head of Google Ventures has said that the Singularity, when AI exceeds human intelligence, opens the door to a future where we could "upload" ourselves into a robot or new younger human. Ray predicts the Singularity in 2045. What do you think about this possibility? Given the exponential nature of computers and AI, it is reasonable to believe that a superhuman intelligence will indeed be created. The question then is what will happen next.

Another area where AI is being used and will become widespread is in robot assisted or entirely robotic surgery. For example, a 2017 study showed that robot guided spine surgery using AI helped reduce complications by five times over doctor only surgeries.[65] The da Vinci System is an AI guided surgical robot system that is already used in heart, intestinal, head and neck and urinary surgeries. da Vinci has greatly enhanced minimally invasive surgery that allows faster recovery and much smaller cuts to the human body.[66] The system was approved for patient use in 2000 and was initially used for prostate removals. In 2016, an announcement was made about what may be the first fully autonomous AI driven surgery on the bowel of a pig by the STAR system tested by the Children's National Health System and Johns Hopkins.[67] Forbes magazine even predicted back in 2017 that surgeons would be replaced one day.[68] As you would expect, the pace

---

[65] https://www.thespinejournalonline.com/article/S1529-9430(17)30851-3/fulltext
[66] https://www.davincisurgery.com/da-vinci-systems/about-da-vinci-systems
[67] https://www.newsweek.com/2016/05/20/robot-soft-tissue-surgery-pig-bowels-455765.html
[68] https://www.forbes.com/sites/haroldstark/2017/07/10/prepare-yourselves-robots-will-soon-replace-doctors-in-healthcare/#47387bde52b5

of approval from the government for fully autonomous robotic surgery will be quite slow, as no one would want to push out this technology before it is ready, but one day perhaps soon it will happen. Would you let a robot do your surgery?

Another logical use for AI in medicine is answering routine queries over the phone, by e-mail or by text message. Don't think an AI can interact with humans in a natural way to answer such questions? Then check out Google's AI Assistant making an appointment for a haircut back in early 2018, and the technology has advance considerably in the two years since then.[69] It is beyond doubt now that your home AI device (Alexa, Google Home, etc.) will soon be making routine appointments for you and managing your calendar and run your schedule autonomously at your request. An early-stage example of a partially manual AI to help manage your calendar is TrevorAI.[70] See what you think! Does it make managing your calendar easier? Would you turn over your schedule management to an AI rather than yourself or an assistant? Like most new technology, it all depends on reliability. But my point is, if AI already exist that can call someone and make an appointment or help manage your calendar, then an AI to answer routine medical questions from consumers in a fully automated way is already in progress. The technology to do so either exists or is being matured right now.

As discussed in Chapter 6, possibly the coolest medical potential use for AI is the brain-computer interface (BCI). We already discussed its impact on work in the future. What about in medicine? Well, let's say that you have the nanobots

---

[69] https://futurism.com/google-assistant-booked-haircut-duplex
[70] https://www.trevorai.com/

in your body, and they detect an anomaly in a cell. The nanobot reaches out to a cancer database to check for matches through your BCI. The results come back that the anomaly is not cancer. Whew! If it did match something in the cancer database, the nanobot would alert your doctor through the BCI, while your home AI automatically makes an appointment for you for further evaluation and treatment. In this example, the very early detection and treatment of a problem has the potential to save millions of lives. With that in mind, would you get a BCI? What if your BCI, knowing what you are about to eat, had your home AI tell you that it's better to have a more nutritious alternative snack that would help a deficiency in your body at the moment, say of a particular vitamin. Would that entice you to get a BCI? Many people are understandably nervous about such a foreign device being put into their body. But like many other things, the next generation would not have that reluctance, and doing it would become widespread.

There is an astounding amount of work being done today around AI and medicine/healthcare. It is impossible to cover a lot of it in a beginning guide like this book. For a deeper dive, search the internet for a particular disease with AI, and fascinating articles will come up. By the way, with your BCI you only need to think it. No more finding the phone or going to the computer, typing the question and sifting results. The results appear right on your Augmented Reality contact lenses for your review. Those are almost here already. Check out the company called Mojo Vision.[71]

---

[71] https://www.fastcompany.com/90441928/the-making-of-mojo-ar-contact-lenses-that-give-your-eyes-superpowers

# AI and Robots

A natural use of AI today is in robotics. When I think about the future of AI-driven robotics, I think about The Terminator. However, likely applications in this area will be helpful to humans rather than trying to destroy us. So, when do you think that the first robot was invented? Maybe the 1950's? Nope. The first known robot was invented between 400 and 350 BCE by the mathematician Archytas and was an artificial bird. The bird was made of wood and was steam powered.[72] Archytas is considered the father of mechanical engineering. In Chapter 6 I talked about George Devol creating the first practical robot for manufacturing in the 1950's, so even though there were a lot of people thinking about robots over the last 2,000 years including DaVinci, their practical uses to make tasks easier and more efficient are relatively new.

Well, Chapter 6 talked about robotics at work. But robots will have broad applicability outside of work. I briefly mentioned the Toyota Research robot that is being trained to perform household tasks. But household robots are already here and in use. Robotic vacuums have been around since 1996, but they didn't work well and were discontinued. In 2002, iRobot launched the Roomba, which quickly became a big success.[73] In 2005, iRobot launched the Scooba floor washing robot. By 2017, iRobot had sold a stunning 20 million home robots.[74]

---

[72] http://www.todayifoundout.com/index.php/2010/10/the-first-known-robot-was-created-around-400-bc-and-was-a-mechanical-bird/
[73] https://www.irobot.com/about-irobot/company-information/history
[74] https://www.irobot.com/about-irobot/company-information/history

iRobot now has dozens of competitors. These home robots have been steadily improved by all vendors to clean better and better. The Roomba 980 includes "intelligent visual navigation", i.e. AI. iRobot also sells robot pool cleaners, commercial robots and a wide range of military/security robots. These robots will continue to evolve quickly based on hardware and AI improvements.

One of the most well-known current robot companies using AI is Boston Dynamics. They make four different models of robots for various purposes including Spot for hazardous environments, Handle for the warehouse, and Pick for loading and unloading trucks and more.[75] Another company called Dronesense uses AI to make drones fly autonomously in military and public safety situations.[76] NASA is working directly with industry to create airspace rules so that drones are allowed to fly autonomously. Of course, there is Rethink Robotic's Sawyer robot that has become very popular in manufacturing and uses AI to be quickly trained to assist in making products.[77] Piaggio Fast Forward's robots assist people with carrying things while following along behind them using AI.[78] This is a retail shopping application. UIPath's digital robots are using AI to become independent of humans while assisting online consumers.[79] Hanson Robotics has become famous for its AI-driven interactive robots who can have natural conversations with humans.[80] This is the current equivalent of Jarvis on Iron Man who answers questions for humans.

---

[75] https://www.bostondynamics.com/
[76] https://www.dronesense.com/
[77] https://www.rethinkrobotics.com/
[78] https://www.piaggiofastforward.com/
[79] https://www.uipath.com/product/robots
[80] https://www.hansonrobotics.com/

The most likely place that you will soon see or have seen a robot is a retail store. For example, I was recently in a Stop 'n Shop grocery store, and a robot followed me around for a few minutes to see if I was shoplifting. It was an odd experience the first time. On the other hand, it may have been a rolling kiosk designed to answer questions and locate products. Or both. Lowe's has its LoweBot robot that will identify an item visually and take the customer to it if it is in stock. The LoweBot also takes inventory.[81] Simbe makes an inventory robot that has been tested by Target and is used in Schnucks grocery stores.[82]

Pretty soon you will see Softbank's Pepper robot in stores. Pepper helps you find items in stores, greets you and answers questions about what you are looking for.[83] I saw one at the Applied AI Conference in San Francisco in 2018, and it was very cute and interactive. Softbank has also partnered with Simbe to sell Simbe's Tally inventory robot through Softbank's sales channel.[84] Softbank also has a commercial AI-driven vacuum cleaner called Whiz that autonomously cleans malls, office buildings and other public spaces.[85] Softbank, as part of a global conglomerate with a Vision Fund for investment of $100 billion, has the strength to dominate the robot space in retail if it does it properly.[86]

In another retail example, Best Buy is using a Chloe robot to deliver items needing security to customers in the store.

---

[81] https://www.lowesinnovationlabs.com/lowebot
[82] https://www.simberobotics.com/
[83] https://www.softbankrobotics.com/us/pepper
[84] https://www.therobotreport.com/softbank-simbe-retail-robotics/
[85] https://www.softbankrobotics.com/
[86] https://www.reuters.com/article/us-softbank-elliott-vision-fund-idUSKCN20M22A

These items include video games, game consoles and controllers, as well as movies, TV shows and music on DVD's (how quaint).[87] As you might guess, these are high theft items, and customers pay and then Chloe delivers the order to the customer. This robot has been in testing at Best Buy's Chelsea store since 2015. Chloe offers 24-hour service there in a lobby like an ATM does.

A final case for robots in retail is delivery, which we also talked about in chapter 7. The Domino's Robotic Unit, rebranded DOM, has been in testing in Australia. As Domino's says on their website, DOM "is able to navigate from starting point to destination, selecting the best path to travel and his on-board sensors enable him to perceive obstacles along the way and avoid them if necessary." This is an AI-driven robot to deliver your hot pizza! DOM is also now an ordering chatbot.[88] In Chapter 5, I discussed other efforts at autonomous delivery already happening on college campuses and elsewhere today. So, robots in retail help answer questions, make recommendations, manage inventory and even make deliveries, all with the help of AI. The sophistication of these robots is all just at the beginning of what is possible.

There are obviously many other potential uses of robots driven by AI. One of the most interesting examples today is the ANA Avatar XPrize. The XPrize was founded by Peter Diamandis to drive forward cutting-edge technology that isn't currently in existence but would have a profound impact on society at large. The ANA Avatar XPrize "is a four-year global competition focused on the development of an Avatar

---

[87] https://www.dmnews.com/customer-experience/article/13035435/retail-review-best-buys-chloe
[88] https://www.dominos.com/chat-pizza-order/

System that will transport a human's sense, actions and presence to a remote location in real time, leading to a more connected world."[89] This XPrize is an example of robotics at its best.

---

[89] https://www.xprize.org/prizes/avatar

# AI and Energy

AI will impact all aspects of the energy industry, from oil companies to traditional energy generators to renewable energy generators to transmission facilities to consumers. In fact, experts say the entire energy production and distribution system will change, and within the decade of the 2020's. For example, at the Applied AI Conference in San Francisco in 2018, the new ventures director from E.on utility in Germany was a speaker, and he said that the electricity grid will wholly change within the next ten years. Currently, the electrical system in the U.S. primarily includes traditional power generation stations using coal, oil, natural gas or nuclear, as well as hydroelectric power from dams. The generated power is then distributed through major transmission lines that are regionally structured over large areas, for example the whole eastern U.S. Then the power is routed over local distribution lines from distribution facilities to individual commercial or residential customers. This large top-down distribution system will be replaced by small area systems, primarily through renewable power generation and local battery farms to smooth out the inconsistencies of renewable power, all monitored and driven by AI. In this way, instead of large areas losing power, only small areas with much fewer customers would have an outage at any given time. Very similar language appears on the Consolidated Edison website, the utility that I get my power from here in the U.S. So, the restructuring of generation, transmission and distribution is a global phenomenon occurring with the major utilities in all the advanced countries, and AI will play a significant role in managing the future grid. In developing countries still needing electricity, they will leapfrog the U.S. model straight to the new distributed model.

As a great example of current changes to the electrical generation and storage paradigm, let's look at the story of Southern California Edison (SCE) and Tesla. Tesla signed an agreement in 2016 to provide what at that time was the largest battery storage array at a substation in the world at SCE's Mira Loma facility. The Powerpacks, unveiled in 2017, store the equivalent of hundreds of acres of solar power in the small space of the substation.[90] The reason that utilities need storage capacity is that solar panels only generate power when the sun is shining, although that is changing now. Utilities need to be able to store the extra electricity generated during the day for use during the night or on cloudy days. Similarly, wind power only generates on windy days, and storage is needed to save the power for times when the wind is not blowing enough to keep the power generation going. Effective use of renewable power generation must include storage of electricity for peak load times or times when the renewable sources are not generating any power. This stored power must be held until a time of peak demand on the system or when renewables are not generating power, and an AI can monitor the grid to determine when to release stored power.

The fastest growing storage type is lithium-ion batteries. These are the types of batteries found in electric cars and increasingly for household consumer use. As discussed in the preceding paragraph, lithium-ion batteries are also used for utility-scale storage of electricity. However, there are other types of power storage including molten salt, advanced lead acid (the traditional battery type), flow batteries and non-

---

[90] https://www.businessinsider.com/tesla-powerpack-southern-california-edison-battery-storage-mira-loma-2017-1?op=1

battery storage.[91] For example, in March 2020, a merger was announced between redT energy of the UK and Avalon Battery Corporation of the U.S. This merger will create a large-scale battery company with batteries based on vanadium flow technology.[92] The new company, Invinity Energy Systems, states that their batteries will last 20-25 years versus only 3-5 years for lithium-ion batteries. Molten salt is currently the largest installed base of utility storage.[93] Molten salt technology is much cheaper and more available than lithium is.[94] GE is one of the big players in molten salt technology. It will take some time for the utility scale storage market to mature and narrow down to the best combination of durability and cost.

AI is key to regulating the storage and discharge of battery power regardless of type. The largest player in the lithium battery segment is Tesla, who teamed up with Panasonic to create the Gigafactory. Ground was broken on the first factory in June 2014 in Sparks, Nevada. The Gigafactory 1 is still only about 30 percent complete and produces all batteries for the Model 3 car line and the Tesla Powerpack and Powerwall storage products. Gigafactory 1 is already 1.9 million square feet in size and produces the energy equivalent of 20 GWh per year, which is enough power to run an incredible 14.5 million homes a year.[95] That is astounding! Gigafactory 2 is in Buffalo, New York and was started in

---

[91] https://seekingalpha.com/article/4167555-companies-to-benefit-from-stationary-energy-storage-boom
[92] https://www.edie.net/news/8/Total-to-launch-France-s-largest-energy-storage-project/
[93] https://seekingalpha.com/article/4167555-companies-to-benefit-from-stationary-energy-storage-boom
[94] https://www.betterworldsolutions.eu/smart-grid-battery-molten-salt-battery/
[95] https://www.tesla.com/gigafactory

2017. By 2019, it was producing solar panels, the Tesla Solar Roof, Powerwalls and Powerpacks at this facility.[96] Tesla made Gigafactory 3 in Shanghai, China official in 2018 and completed construction in only two years. The factory is already in production of Model 3 cars.[97] There are at least five other meaningful lithium-ion battery manufacturers though including Samsung and LG, so expect competition to be fierce in this rapidly growing segment.

Months ago, in March 2020, in addition to the announcement of the Invinity merger, Total of France announced the largest energy storage project in French history. This project will be 25MW in size, enough to power 25,000 homes.[98] This project is a good indication of the major changes going on in the energy industry broadly, as Total is one of the largest oil companies in the world and is now working in the energy storage area. Look for more oil companies to change their business model as oil and gas use declines on the rising tide of renewable energy. Also, large industrial companies are getting into the energy storage game including ABB, AES, Enel, Siemens and SolarEdge, representing companies from around the world.[99]

But what about AI in the energy sector or in energy storage? Stem is an example of a company working directly with utilities and large industrial users with an AI solution to

---

[96] https://www.tesla.com/gigafactory2
[97] https://www.dailymail.co.uk/news/article-7587835/Teslas-China-Gigafactory-Huge-2billion-plant-begin-production-days.html
[98] https://www.edie.net/news/8/Total-to-launch-France-s-largest-energy-storage-project/
[99] https://seekingalpha.com/article/4167555-companies-to-benefit-from-stationary-energy-storage-boom

manage their energy use, storage and costs.[100] Also, SAP and Accenture have teamed up to provide an AI-driven system to run oil refineries and pipelines, with the goal of making refining and transport operations more efficient and profitable due to very complex facilities that are difficult for humans to manage well.[101] According to the Utility Analytics Institute, a power company think tank, AI will completely change the current utility business model. Power and energy use will become distributed and local, with local renewable generation, local storage and AI managing demand.[102] AI is right now making existing utilities more profitable by better forecasting demand and reducing losses incurred in the hedging markets. Energy producers and transporters use futures and options on the financial exchanges to manage their risk of sudden price changes in product between the time it is generated and delivered. Whether they lose money on these hedges is dependent on forecasting demand accurately. The oil and gas business do the same thing. AI can forecast much better than humans because the forecast can incorporate much more data.

According to UtilityDive, AI is already in use in a number of ways at utilities, even before the big changes it will drive in the future. Self-healing grids driven by AI re-route power when a local failure occurs. Machine Learning manages the big data from smart meters, smart thermostats, and generation stations. The next frontier will be predicting grid failures based on use and maintenance patterns. Smart

---

[100] https://www.stem.com/
[101] https://www.marketwatch.com/press-release/the-ai-eye-accenture-sap-co-develop-solution-for-oil-gas-companies-2020-03-20
[102] https://utilityanalytics.com/2019/09/ais-action-and-impact-on-the-energy-sector/

appliances will have AI in them in the home, going far beyond the current home assistant. Finally, AI can take over a lot of customer interactions as voice recognition gets better and better, and the AI can check for problems instantaneously while on the phone with a customer about that problem.[103]

So, there are huge changes coming to one of the most fundamental industries of modern life. Power is critical to everything now that our society is totally driven by computers. The decentralization of the power grid into local nodes over time will prevent the kind of large-scale regional blackouts that have had a big impact previously, such as the massive eastern U.S. blackout in 2003 that shut down the Northeast and eastern Canada for two weeks. Many experts believe that power will get much cheaper in the future as well as more reliable as the cost of solar panels and batteries continue to fall, and new technologies continue to come up in this age of exponential change.

---

[103] https://www.utilitydive.com/news/with-artificial-intelligence-its-a-brave-new-world-for-utilities/511008/

# AI and Agriculture

The AI revolution is already well underway in agriculture and food production, distribution and even how it's served in public. In farming, limited efforts at self-driving tractors go all the way back to 2011.[104] In fact, John Deere, the huge global US-based equipment company, has been working on a fully autonomous tractor since the 1990's. But their equipment still requires a farmer to be in the driver's seat after twenty years.[105] That said, Deere's self-steering technology is already about 15 years old![106] Deere's tractors follow a pattern once a human programs it or shows the system where to plow by making the first pass around the edge of a field, and then the tractor takes over and does the rest of the field. GPS makes highly accurate driving possible.[107] All of the above is a consequence of AI bringing self-driving to reality. So, Deere was years ahead of Google, Uber and Tesla in self-driving technology.

Deere has been focusing also on AI to manage the implements the tractor pulls by greatly increasing accuracy of fertilizer and pesticide application, for example. They have partnered with Taranis to help completely manage fields by looking at crop emergence, uneven growth and pests

---

[104] https://modernfarmer.com/2013/04/this-tractor-drives-itself/
[105] https://qz.com/1042343/after-trying-to-build-self-driving-tractors-for-more-than-20-years-john-deere-has-learned-a-hard-truth-about-autonomy/
[106] https://www.cbsnews.com/news/farmers-reap-benefits-self-driving-tractor-technology/
[107] https://www.washingtonpost.com/news/the-switch/wp/2015/06/22/google-didnt-lead-the-self-driving-vehicle-revolution-john-deere-did/

attacking crops.[108] The platform currently manages millions of acres in five countries! Like all AI, it learns as it grows and has more data and is getting better all the time at identifying problems in its monitored fields. Taranis is an Israeli company. Taranis uses Deep Learning to become more and more accurate in identifying specific crop diseases and pests, and usually a few growing seasons are needed to fully train the AI.[109] Israel has a relatively long history in AI going back at least to the 2000's and most likely earlier. In 2017, Israel had 430 AI startups and at least 17 featured companies working in many industry sectors with AI applications.[110]

News of the first production fully self-driving (no human) tractor debuted in October 2018, and boy is it a beauty! The Valtra H202 is a hydrogen powered tractor that can run day and night autonomously, so that will significantly speed up farm work.[111] The tractor still can be driven by a human in difficult terrain or tight spaces, but it can work fully autonomously. All prior tractors or combines (harvesters) needed a human in the cabin. Of course, other tractor companies are in mid- to late development with fully self-driving tractors, like Case IH. Case defines two types of autonomy, with Category 4: Supervised Autonomy where the operator is not in the tractor but remains in the field to monitor it and intervene if necessary. Category 5: Full

---

[108] https://taranis.ag/
[109] https://www.forbes.com/sites/lanabandoim/2019/04/27/how-self-driving-tractors-and-ai-are-changing-agriculture/#751f6147fa14
[110] https://www.israel21c.org/17-israeli-companies-pioneering-artificial-intelligence/
[111] https://www.therichest.com/lifestyles/self-driving-tractor-future-farming/

Autonomy is either remote control or AI control.[112] Kubota likewise defines Level 2 as semi-autonomous and launched their AgriRobo tractor in 2017, but they literally a few months ago (April 2020) debuted their fully autonomous Level 3 concept tractor that is in development featuring AI.[113] Tractors are not the only farm equipment on this path. Combine harvesters are coming along the path of autonomy typically only a year behind tractors. For example, most semi-autonomous tractors were out in 2017 (although Deere was years ahead this date), and many semi-autonomous combines came out in 2018 (Case and Kubota). Combines have advanced rapidly through AI by using Deep Learning to recognize the grain being harvested and make sure that it is not being damaged by the combine. AI can make changes to the equipment in real time to ensure the highest possible yield through preventing damage and waste.[114]

Implements like pesticide and herbicide applicators are well down the AI track as well. For example, John Deere bought Blue River, a Machine Learning startup, in 2017 to drive their AI automation across their farm equipment portfolio. With applicators specifically, Deep Learning has reduced pesticide use by 80-90% in a few years by using advanced vision, sensors and AI to change application from the whole field down to individual plants.[115] Other applicators are used to

---

[112] https://www.caseih.com/northamerica/en-us/innovations/automation
[113] https://www.farmweekly.com.au/story/6707850/kubota-shows-what-is-to-come/
[114] https://www.forbes.com/sites/bernardmarr/2019/03/15/the-amazing-ways-john-deere-uses-ai-and-machine-vision-to-help-feed-10-billion-people/#584f1dc02ae9
[115] https://www.forbes.com/sites/bernardmarr/2019/03/15/the-amazing-ways-john-deere-uses-ai-and-machine-vision-to-help-feed-10-billion-people/#584f1dc02ae9

apply fertilizer or water. Finally, regarding farm implements, AI-driven planters are in development that will save significantly on seed costs.[116] These advancements are critical to offset the declining population engaged in farming through increased efficiency and the need to feed 10 billion people on Earth by 2050 through higher productivity and lower costs.

Meanwhile, the whole concept of the traditional farm is changing. AeroFarms is a global company building out vertical farms in urban settings to provide fresh vegetables to traditionally underserved communities like Newark, NJ. AeroFarms uses predictive analytics (AI) to monitor each plant each day consisting of millions of data points per day.[117] This type of farming improves many things, including much lower transportation costs, fresher produce, better land use characteristics and making pesticide free healthy vegetables accessible to all. The vertical farms are also far more productive than a regular farm and much better at conserving water. There are at least five companies since 2017, probably more, offering predictive analytics AI-driven software now.

A lot of effort is going into robot pickers of high value products like grapes and strawberries that are easily damaged in the harvesting process. In addition, these robots are beginning to help offset the shortage of skilled farm labor to pick these crops. One example comes out of France, and it's called Wall-Ye. Wall-Ye is an AI-driven robot that manages plant health in vineyards.[118]

---

[116] https://www.surefireag.com/products
[117] https://aerofarms.com/technology/
[118] https://www.dailymail.co.uk/sciencetech/article-2209975/Meet-Wall-Ye-The-French-grape-picking-robot-work-day-night--vineyard-workers-job.html

Vision Robotics in California has at least four different types of AI-driven robots, including one for the vineyard also.[119] Harvest CROO Robotics is in test to commercialize a robotic strawberry picker that uses AI to determine which berries are ripe and should be picked, and which are not ready yet and should wait for the next pass.[120] Robocrop, developed in the UK, is the world's first AI-driven raspberry picker and can also pick tomatoes and cauliflower. This robot can pick 25,000 raspberries per hour versus 15,000 for an experienced human picker.[121] All of these pickers are virtually brand new on the market or just coming to market, so this is very cutting-edge technology. Things are changing very, very rapidly in farming as we have now moved into the implementation phase of Deep Learning. There are already at least five companies with AI-driven strawberry pickers now, all in the space of a few years.

Finally, let's not leave Africa out! Over 50 percent of Africans are still farmers. Aerobiotics is a South African company that assists farmers with their Aeroview solution, an AI-driven farm management platform that also uses drones and satellites to help farmers maximize their crop yield. Aerobiotics has customers in many African countries, Australia and New Zealand. They offer orchard management, identify problems with trees and also do pest management.[122] Despite challenges with infrastructure in parts of Africa, it has the opportunity to jump straight over several generations of technology as farming improvements are new implementations rather than an expensive upgrade process to

---

[119] https://www.visionrobotics.com/
[120] https://harvestcroo.com/
[121] https://www.theguardian.com/technology/2019/may/26/world-first-fruit-picking-robot-set-to-work-artificial-intelligence-farming
[122] https://www.aerobotics.com/?identifier=default-sign-up-button

established production systems like in the U.S. Africa can leapfrog several steps in the development process this way by focusing on new technologies and especially by fully utilizing AI in these efforts.

# AI and Quantum Computing

A technology that has been in development for decades but is just beginning to reach the point where it will become a new foundation for AI is Quantum Computing. Quantum Computing is based on quantum physics, which extends classical physics down from the atomic level to the sub-atomic level. Put simply, at the classical level of physics, things behave as particles, like atoms and molecules, which combine into the things that we see in our world, including us. These theories began to be developed as early as the 1680's by Sir Isaac Newton and were steadily advanced over the following centuries. Classical physics described matter and energy using calculus and the inputs of mass, movement and force. Most observable phenomenon that we see are explainable by classical physics as now described in the Standard Model of the behavior of physical matter and energy. This physics is what you learn in high school and college if you take it as a general requirement, not as a major.

However, at the quantum or sub-atomic level, matter can behave as a particle (classical physics) or like a wave (quantum physics), wherein the properties of such small matter can change as a result of the act of observing it. For example, light has wave characteristics. For computing purposes, the quantum coding is not just binary with a 1 or 0 like traditional computers, but also includes variations called superposition and entanglement. Traditional computing always has a 1 or a 0 in the same position at all times on the chip. Quantum Computing can have the values in multiple positions. But at the time and point of measurement, the code must become a 0 or 1. The theory of quantum matter was first described by Albert Einstein's General Theory of Relativity in 1905. To date, there is no unifying theory between the Standard Model and General Relativity. That is one of the "holy grails" of physics, a unified theory to explain everything regardless of size in the universe.

Quantum Computing has the potential to be orders of magnitude faster than traditional computing for certain tasks. In October 2019, once again very recently, Google AI and NASA jointly published a paper proclaiming that "Quantum Supremacy" had been achieved. What does this mean? For one specific mathematical problem, a quantum computer solved that problem very quickly, where a traditional computer would take at least 10,000 years to solve it. So, for that particular problem, the quantum computer was far better than a traditional computer. While this event is a breakthrough, the current biggest problem with Quantum Computing is high error rates, far higher than a traditional computer. One reason for this error rate is simply less time in development. At the start of the book, we talked about traditional computers as we know them today being completed during World War II in the late 1930's and early 1940's. Traditional computers have then been around for 80 years now. In contrast, even though the theory of a quantum computer was laid out in the early 1980's by Paul Benioff, practical work on such a computer really began in the late 1990's, or only a little over 20 years ago. Interestingly, this timing roughly mirrors AI in many respects.

Why is Quantum Computing important to AI? Because as algorithms get more and more sophisticated, more and more computing power is required to run them. At all times, traditional computing has a practical computational limit of time. Some problems would take so long to solve using classical computing that it is of no use. Quantum Computing, once fully working, will have a much, much higher limit in terms of speed (time) to solve very complex analyses, and therefore would allow AI to progress far beyond the capabilities of a traditional computing architecture. So, the development of AI and Quantum Computing go hand in hand in this respect. Some experts predict that within five years quantum computers will have advanced to the point of driving significantly more powerful AI.[123] That is because a quantum computer can process multiple possibilities at once where a traditional computer has to solve problems linearly. In this same article, Microsoft says that a quantum computer can train Machine Learning algorithms "exponentially faster" than a traditional computer with huge quantities of data. So, between the much higher computing power and much greater speed, quantum computers are a natural fit to amplify the effects of AI going forward. Commercial quantum computers are not yet available though, and some of them require cooling to astronomically low temperatures close to absolute zero (-460 degrees Fahrenheit or -273 degrees Celsius – to point at which matter stops moving). That requirement puts the air conditioning needs of current computers to shame.

We have talked several times in this book about needing large quantities of data to "train" AI algorithms to identify a pattern and find relationships within those patterns. This data must be "structured" in that the variables within the data have to be very precisely defined and catalogued. We have also talked about AI needing huge computing power to run these programs. A human can only identify relationships between obvious factors. AI on a classical computer can see relationships within large data sets that are not obvious to humans because they are subtle. Therefore, AI on a classical

---

[123] https://www.wsj.com/articles/when-quantum-computing-meets-ai-smarter-digital-assistants-and-more-11558631925

computer can find answers to problems that humans cannot. Quantum Computing can see even more relationships. Why? Because it can work with a far higher number of variables. For example, on April 14, 2020, an article appeared about using AI and Quantum Computing to solve coronavirus problems like treatment and vaccination. In this article, a Quantum Computing startup called D-Wave Systems says it is giving free access to its platform of combined supercomputing and quantum computing to "precisely solve highly complex problems with up to 10,000 fully connected variables."[124] This complexity of computing capacity is wholly new. Quantum Computing therefore will surface relationships in data that even classical supercomputing cannot find. This article does mention that Quantum Computing is just emerging as a viable technology, i.e., it is just beginning to work in a practical way on practical problems.

Some believe that one of the strongest early markets for Quantum Computing is healthcare. This is because healthcare datasets are growing exponentially, and more powerful computing will dramatically impact this industry. How? Faster development of new drugs, faster identification on new diseases, faster strategies to stop the spread of viruses, and faster diagnosis of disease in humans. It is difficult to predict the future in this area because humans currently have no real experience with the coming power of Quantum Computing and limited experience with the power of AI. Humans' ability to predict the future in these situations has a very poor record later when looking back. However, we can all understand that if you increase computing power by 1,000 times that it will have a very dramatic impact. It is like the caveman days

---

[124] https://www.forbes.com/sites/gilpress/2020/04/14/calling-on-ai-and-quantum-computing-to-fight-the-coronavirus/#2162916266c4

versus now. The eventual impact may be that big. We can know that these two technologies will drive huge change without knowing how that change will play out over time.

While AI is being rapidly adopted by companies with huge IT budgets (like the Fortune 100), its adoption by the mid-size and small companies will highly depend on it becoming more affordable. In the tech world, a new technology is hugely expensive at the start. Think of flat screen TV's. In 2000, a flat screen of a common size in homes today was $5,000 or more each. Today you can get one for several hundred dollars. The same will happen in computing. As Quantum Computing gradually goes mainstream in the tech world, the cost of classical computing sufficient to run AI algorithms will come down dramatically over time. As computing cost drops further, then small and mid-size businesses will be able to adopt AI more and more. Large companies of course will move on to Quantum Computing, allowing further dramatic gains in efficiency and customer experience. Therefore, we can expect to see Quantum Computing advance significantly over the next ten years, and AI penetration to then move strongly into the smaller markets using cheaper and cheaper classical computing.

What does this mean to the future then, this powerful combination of AI and Quantum Computing? Used wisely, it opens the door to solving humanity's most difficult problems, like providing water and food to all, addressing climate change, curing intractable diseases and much more. The potential power of these technologies is to usher in a new age for mankind. Used wrongly, these technologies present great dangers. The obvious ones are new weapons development that have no reliable defense, thereby opening the door to a strike on another country with that country having no practical way to defend itself. This possibility then leads to a new and potentially more deadly arms race than the nuclear one. Another possibility is a further concentration of wealth to an even smaller few with no viable options for the rest of humanity to feed, clothe and shelter itself. The future is coming. It is up to all of us to insist that these transformative technologies are used constructively and for the benefit of the many, and many organizations like AI for Good are already working to make sure that these technologies benefit rather than harm humanity.

# AI and 3D Printing

3D printing, just like AI, will be changing the world. In fact, these are two "converging technologies" as Peter Diamandis says. So, what really is 3D printing? Well, 3D printing is also called additive manufacturing. What does that mean? Traditional manufacturing would be called subtractive. For example, you take a block of metal or wood and cut away pieces until you get the shape of the object you are trying to make. 3D printing or additive manufacturing is the opposite. You take a material and build it up layer by layer in the desired shape until you get the final shape that you are looking for.

What are the advantages of 3D printing? There are many, but we will talk about a few of them. First, the amount of waste in the manufacturing process is much, much lower. In normal manufacturing, high volumes of waste are created from all the excess material being removed from the item. In 3D printing, waste is near zero. For the manufacture of titanium aircraft parts for example, waste is far less, the speed is a third faster at 100 units and energy use is a small fraction of that of normal manufacturing.[125] So, the advantages outlined here are first, less waste; second, less time to make; and third, far less energy use for smaller quantity orders.

What are the advantages of traditional manufacturing by comparison? The biggest advantage for traditional manufacturing is volume. 3D printing today is too slow for high volume applications. If for example you needed 1,000 pieces of an object (rather than just 100), it would take far too

---

[125] https://www.digitalalloys.com/blog/comparison-additive-manufacturing-cnc-machining/

long to produce them through 3D printing today. The effect is magnified at higher volumes like 10,000 pieces. It is difficult to tell how 3D printers will advance in the coming years regarding their inherent volume limitations. However, many experts believe that mass 3D printing will drive the consumer market away from mass consumption and toward individualized consumption for many goods. This means that instead of a company making 150,000 pairs of a certain type of jeans, people will make them individually on their home 3D printer from a pattern bought over the internet. In this way, the profit comes from the pattern (or intellectual property) instead of actually making the product.

Where does AI come into the 3D printing picture? 3D printing is a complex process. Much of the early printers required trial and error to get them to work correctly to make a particular item. This type of process is very time consuming. As 3D printer software advances, more and more AI is being programmed into it, particularly Machine Learning. In this way, the printer can "learn" to make things through its own iterative process in the software. An example is software from a French company called Sculpteo that reads CAD (computer aided design) files, optimizes them and then formulates the best 3D printing process.[126] AI-driven software could eventually eliminate the trial and error involved in developing a new part. At that point, AI makes 3D printing simple and easy for even home use.

AI can drive improvement in three other areas of 3D printing. AI can improve defect detection, reproducibility of parts and the invention of wholly new materials. As we talked about in other chapters, improvements in sensors coupled

---

[126] https://emerj.com/ai-sector-overviews/artificial-intelligence-applications-additive-manufacturing-3d-printing/

with AI can greatly improve quality in manufacturing. This is defect detection. Reproducibility of parts means being able to make the part exactly the same each time in volume. In traditional manufacturing, a machine called a CNC is used to remove the excess material to get the finished shape. It uses a program to cut off the same material time after time. Similarly, AI can be used to control the material addition to make sure that it is identical from part to part in 3D printing. Finally, AI can be used to formulate new materials, for 3D printing or otherwise, to make products that are superior to anything available today for a specific application. In truth, AI will revolutionize materials in a way that has never been seen in human history, and it is already happening. New materials are entering the market now that have 50% longer wear for a purpose than current materials, which reduces the cost over time of using the material for a product.

What is the future of 3D printing? Many experts believe that 3D printing will become huge in the medical field. In a mind-blowing development, human tissues and organs are now being 3D printed. What does this mean? For someone on a transplant list waiting for an organ, it gives them an alternative to transplant as it is today. It can also mean life. Twenty people die each day waiting for an organ, and there are over 112,000 people on the transplant list right now in the U.S. alone.[127] 3D printing uses the patient's own tissue to minimize complications. 3D printed prosthetics are also starting to reduce the cost of these specialized devices and improve how they work, which gives people with major limb loss an improved quality of life. 3D printing is also aiding in cheaper and better surgical tools, pharmaceutical design and

---

[127] https://www.organdonor.gov/statistics-stories/statistics.html

dental implants, among other things.[128] AI drives many of these new printers, and the Aether Bioprinter is a good example of the state-of-the-art in this area.[129]

Another industry where 3D printing is making a growing impact is space-related manufacturing. Many rocket parts today are 3D printed, and both SpaceX and Blue Origin are using the technology. ULA, one of the traditional defense-based contractors, is also using 3D printing for specialty components on their rockets. However, a newcomer to the space launch industry, Relativity Space, is largely manufacturing their rockets with 3D printers, including some the size of whole rooms.[130] There are even plans to take 3D printers to Mars eventually to print rockets there. One reason why 3D printing makes sense for certain rocket parts is that they are complex and low volume. The lower the volume, the less competitive that traditional manufacturing is on cost.

In addition to space, the aircraft industry is also using 3D printing. There are many plastic and metal parts of lower volume in a plane that are ideal for 3D printing. Airbus has over 1,000 parts on a typical plane now made by 3D printers.[131] Boeing is in hot pursuit. Both manufacturers are now working on 3D printing of aircraft interiors. Also, engine components that are a single piece per engine are now routinely made this way. Eos, one of the major players in 3D printing, is working hard to continue pressing forward

---

[128] https://all3dp.com/2/3d-printing-in-medicine-the-best-applications/
[129] https://discoveraether.com/
[130] https://www.relativityspace.com/
[131] https://blog.trimech.com/how-3d-printing-in-transforming-the-aerospace-industry

adoption in the aerospace industry.[132] They are confirming that using 3D printing to build aircraft is improving reliability through fewer parts being combined by using 3D printing and at a much lower cost than the previous manufacturing techniques.

3D printing is also having a major impact in construction. 3D printers have built entire houses and commercial buildings now.[133] In particular, 3D printing is rapidly lowering construction costs for small houses to help homeless people have a home of their own.[134] In fact, a 650 square foot home can be built for as little as $10,000 for the structure, plus plumbing, electric and outfitting. NASA even ran a competition for 3D printers that can build habitats on the Moon and Mars.[135] Austin, TX is building a homeless village using 3D printers.[136] There is even a company called haus.me that is building homes for people in the Southwestern U.S. in 4-8 weeks, shipped from their factory, versus months of traditional construction time. So, 3D printing is driving cost reduction and sustainability of materials in housing and will only accelerate rapidly in the next decade as the technology matures.

3D printers are also making food, wine and other alcoholic beverages. Many foods are now able to be 3D printed. In fact, all the way back in 2015, the world's first restaurant with

---

[132] https://www.eos.info/en/3d-printing-examples-applications/aerospace-3d-printing
[133] https://all3dp.com/1/3d-printed-house-building-construction/
[134] https://www.thezebra.com/resources/home/3d-printed-homes/
[135] https://www.nasa.gov/directorates/spacetech/centennial_challenges/3DPHab/about.html
[136] https://newatlas.com/architecture/3d-printed-low-cost-housing-texas/

only 3D printed food debuted at the London 3D printing show featuring a Michelin star chef.[137] Many foods can now be 3D printed including vegetables and meat. The American Society of Mechanical Engineers (ASME) has even proposed a way to end world hunger through 3D printing of food.[138] 3D printed food is also better for the environment because it incorporates natural things to create tasty food without the heavy environmental impact of traditionally raised meat products.[139]

Finally, the jewelry business is another industry being revolutionized by 3D printing. 3D printing of jewelry is much faster, cheaper and often of higher quality than traditional casting of jewelry. 3D printing is taking over the design and casting processes, while finishing is still done by hand.[140] Multiple copies of a particular design can be generated rapidly, and hand finished for popular pieces. The 3D printing process allows creativity to still be a big part of the jewelry business while making mass produced pieces scale quickly with far less waste. Conversely, for custom jewelry, a jeweler and customer can develop a custom design and make a physical piece to try on in only an hour to see if the final piece will meet the customer's expectation. Indeed, as mentioned at the beginning of the chapter, 3D printing is the great enabler of the truly individualistic consumer.

Why am I talking so much about 3D printing? Almost all printers incorporate AI. AI is used in the design phase, the

---

[137] https://www.foodandwine.com/news/first-restaurant-serve-only-3d-printed-food
[138] https://www.asme.org/topics-resources/content/solving-world-hunger-3dprinted-food
[139] https://3dprinting.com/food/
[140] https://formlabs.com/blog/3d-printed-jewelry/

printing phase and the quality phase of 3D printing to ensure that the final piece matches the design and is of the intended quality. AI makes designing easy and allows exact repeatability in the manufacturing process, which is a constant challenge with traditional manufacturing in the form of quality problems and waste. AI is the driving and enabling technology behind the success of 3D printing, thus the comment at the start of the chapter about converging technologies between AI and 3D.

# Conclusion

Even though AI is 65 years old, it really didn't start impacting society generally until the last 5-10 years. This long "growing up" period was caused by limited computing power and episodic funding for the technology. All that has changed since 2015. Unlimited, affordable computing power is now available along with more capital for startups and high growth companies that any other time in history. The result is a surge in the development and use of AI in recent years. AI was on the long gentle slope of the exponential curve all these years but is now on the start of the steep part of the curve where things really take off.

There is now a lot of talk about the looming heavy job losses that AI will cause. In the past, new technologies have led to the creation of new jobs that replaced the ones that were lost, but after a transition period. That transition period is always intense as displaced workers must learn new skills to adapt to the changed job market. Identifying and learning those new skills takes time for human beings.

However, this time may be different than prior history. The steam engine, railroads, electricity, interstate highways and computers did bring about great change, but it was gradual. The AI revolution will be exponential in speed. The challenge will be to keep up with a rate of change that is itself exponentially increasing now. This unprecedented rate of change will be a unique challenge. Proper management of the AI revolution will take *active* management, not the passive "let's see what happens and react" approach typical of government and institutions. China's approach is illustrative of a planned, focused and funded approach to dominate this new technology. The U.S. has been gradually losing its preeminence in world affairs for years now as the rest of the world develops and as Europe slowly becomes more cohesive and powerful. A lack of planning and management of this AI revolution in the U.S. may cap that decline in influence off. How the U.S. responds is a choice, which includes doing nothing and not having a coherent, well executed policy. That is one of the choices. As we know, all choices have consequences. My sole interest here is to educate and empower the public.

The AI revolution will require rethinking certain aspects of society. The are many differing points of view in this area, and I will not get into that discussion in this book. My intention is solely to bring better awareness to the general public, and especially the younger folks who either haven't started their career or are early in it. Awareness is power, because it opens up the mind to possibilities to cope with the coming changes that wouldn't happen without that awareness. As you can see from the broad cross section of industries discussed in this book, AI is already at work in most of the industries that run the world today. AI's impact will be broad and deep. The way to cope with the onrushing future will be to understand AI's foreseeable limitations and stake out careers in relatively protected areas. Those protected areas are all about where the human touch or ingenuity is still required.

The routine tasks of the world are the most vulnerable. If you are doing that type of work, learn a new skill now. Lifelong learning to continue adapting will be your key to the future. I am not talking about the stuff that you learned in school. I am talking about immediately useful skills and knowledge that positively affects making a living or much more. So, learn how to code. Or pursue the arts. Or start your own service business. If you would like to learn more about what careers will be later in the automation cycle, be sure to check out my YouTube channel, The AI Guide, where I highlight potential career paths every week while continuing to bring you the most current events happening in AI today. There is also a good playlist on the history of AI also. So, go check out The AI Guide on YouTube, and please Subscribe and comment. I answer comments daily.

For more resources to help you prepare for an AI-safe career, go to my website www.davidtheaiguide.com.

Made in United States
North Haven, CT
16 January 2023